Grow Yourself, Grow Your Wealth

Prosperity Practices for Faith and Focus

KAREN RUSSO

Grow Yourself, Grow Your Wealth
Prosperity Practices for Faith and Focus
1st Edition

Money Keys Publishing
877.249.0194
MoneyKeysPractices.com
CustomerCare@TheMoneyKeys.com
ISBN: 978-0-9799439-7-3

Cover Design: Alan Singles
Layout: MiniBuk
Manufactured in the USA by MiniBuk.com

Acknowledgments

To my beloved God: Thank you for lighting the way.

To the men and women of *The Money Keys* Community: You inspire me with your spiritual and financial commitment.

To my prayer partners and spiritual mentors: You lift me up.

To my family: Thank you for your unwavering support.

To the big fella: My hero and my lover, you're the best.

"Karen Russo truly understands how to connect spiritual vision with practical financial actions that are required to achieve results. Discover your answer to 'What's the Money for?' and thrive!"

— Sharon Lechter,
international financial expert and best-selling author of
Think and Grow Rich for Women, Outwitting the Devil, Three Feet from Gold and Rich Dad Poor Dad

"The beautiful being I know as Rev. Karen Russo is a faithful servant, student and teacher of universal spiritual principles."

— Michael Bernard Beckwith,
founder Agape International Spiritual Center, featured in the movie *The Secret* & originator of the *Life Visioning Process*

Contents

Prelude

Dear Beloveds,

Congratulations on picking up this book! You're taking an important step forward in your spiritual and financial expansion. Because you've opened to this page, it tells me that you want deeper spiritual faith and greater income, growth and contribution with money. You've come to the right place.

I want to remind you about what is already true: You are already a child of the divine. You are already precious, powerful and prosperous. You are already exactly where you need to be. If you want to go deeper into your experience of the truth of who you are, then this is the place.

This book will help you express who you are both spiritually and financially. These Prosperity Practices have helped thousands of your brothers and sisters across the globe to feel more peaceful, powerful, prosperous and free.

— Reverend Karen

The Money Keys Story

In 2005-2006, I was visioning how my ministry in the world would expand and got a clear idea to explore very deeply how spirituality and money go together. These are two topics that are not often linked and I felt as though their relationship beckoned greater consideration. I also chose to explore this relationship because I saw that people were suffering. I saw spiritual people suffering with money concerns, and I saw people in the wealth-building and real estate workshops being very disconnected from their spirituality. I knew that money and spirituality were not mutually exclusive, and I wanted to know how they might work together.

One of the most profound ideas that emerged from those days of visioning, contemplation and prayer around this message came on a sunny afternoon in Manhattan Beach, Calif. I was with my dear friend and prayer partner Jennifer, and as we talked about what people truly desire in their financial experiences, she blurted out: "It's not about the money… it's: 'What's the money for?' " When people long for greater financial flow, they are always longing for an increase in their capacity to serve, to share and to give. That's the essence of growing the 'Self' as we grow our wealth.

It's not about the money …
it's: What's the money for?

"The Money Keys" is my first book on this topic. It is based on a framework called The Money Map, which explores the idea that we create our wealth. That our wealth happens through us, not to us.

Our experience of wealth and money is created by our spirituality, beliefs and habits. That's where *The Money Keys* book and ministry was born.

The Money Map allows us to see all of the elements in one place so that we can better understand our money life. It helps us to see where we are and visualize what's possible for our money life. The Money Map is a framework for understanding and expanding your entire financial life – both the inner and outer experience of it.

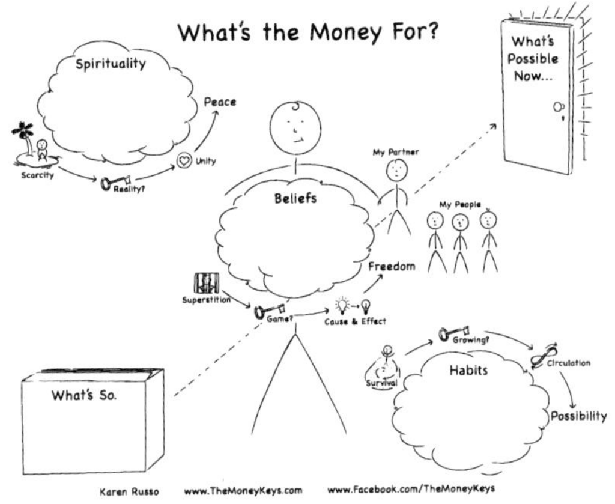

When people understand how their spirituality, beliefs and habits are connected to wealth, they're better able to escape the challenges around money that I call the "money traps." Money traps include scarcity, superstition and survival mode. These challenges create worry or stress about money.

Many believe that more money will eliminate worry and stress about money. Since these upsets are more mental, emotional and spiritual, the answers come from the use of natural laws of being that come from the mental and spiritual, or metaphysical. When you escape the money traps through a deeper, greater understanding of how these laws, or universal principles, apply to wealth, it is possible to create personal and professional financial lives that are peaceful, prosperous, generous and free.

Through my exploration, the experience of writing *The Money Keys* and time spent mentoring and working with people to address their own relationships with spirituality and money, I've discovered that people achieve their spiritual and financial goals more effectively with simple, consistent and conscious weekly activities. Out of that, we created the mindful rituals of observing and caring for money, the practices that I call Prosperity Practices: Money Focus Monday and Spiritual Faith Friday. Each one of these activities was developed by me with the help of students in our global spirituality and money community. Over the last seven years, more than 100,000 people have been touched by the message and a deeper understanding of the connection between spirituality and money. They love to have weekly activities to anchor their growth.

If you enjoyed my first book, *The Money Keys,* or simply want to learn more about the relationship between spirituality and money or how to escape money traps, please visit www.themoneykeys.com. You can access a chapter of the book, audio guide and online tools there. That's also the best place to discover how to become a community member and join your brothers and sisters across the globe in deepening your spiritual faith while you achieve your financial goals.

Why Prosperity Practices?

Spiritual confusion, ambivalence and suffering around money have been age-old issues. Today, with so much uncertainty in the world of finance, it is somewhat common to feel trepidation about money We have found that financial upsets are one of the most destructive issues couples face. We have also found that, particularly with women, people feel even less confident about making financial and investment decisions than in the past.

When people experience a financial loss or betrayal such as a divorce, bankruptcy, foreclosure or job loss, they can experience shame and sadness and feel overwhelmed about how to move forward with money. And it's not only when financial situations are difficult that emotions flare. We have worked with many successful business owners who struggle with doubt, disagreements and feeling overwhelmed as their revenue grows.

There are two universal problems we are working to solve in our relationship with money. One is that when spirituality and money are disconnected, people suffer. The other is that when people don't have consistent action toward their goals, if they lack ways to stay focused on where they are going, they don't make progress. ***A spiritual approach to money directly addresses the issues of spiritual suffering and financial stagnation.*** It helps people feel powerful, prosperous, peaceful and free – regardless of their financial circumstance.

People grow and change through both action and reflection. They also grow by a holistic strategy for change that engages their spirit, emotions, thoughts and actions. Often the best way to create change is to have guidance and support. We have discovered that 80 percent of people will abandon their goals, resolutions or improvement objectives within 30 days. What makes the 20 percent successful? They have an approach that includes a deep commitment to their goals, guidance from a mentor and the support of a group.

The Prosperity Practices are a way to address the problems each of us might have with changing our experience of money. Our time, energy and attention are powerful forces when we tap into and make use of them. When we invest in a weekly activity that keeps us focused and faithful, we accelerate our results.

The Prosperity Practices allow us to address our own personal money concerns within the framework of *The Money Keys* and the Money Map. Without something like a wealth ritual, without a consistent way to focus your attention, most people, we have found, will replicate their past experiences. They may choose or re-choose the same thoughts, the same choices and the same level of consciousness that they have in the past unless they have both 1) a deep desire to change and 2) a way to change. Human beings, ever creatures of habit, will continue to have the same experiences over and over unless they create an inspiring destination and a practical plan.

Prosperity Practices

Let's take just a moment to better understand Prosperity Practices as rituals. As we have learned, it is highly unlikely that you will make a real change unless you have a good reason, a way to get to your goal and a group of people who will support you. These three elements are vital to creating change. A ritual, according to the Merriam Webster Dictionary, is: Something "always done in a particular situation and in the same way each time." We often think of it as a consistent action taken with intentional or deliberate consciousness or a consistent action with a chosen attitude.

We perform rituals more often than we might realize in our daily lives. Often we do them with the intent to pass on information.

When you learned the ABCs song or your multiplication tables, you performed the ritual of repeating it, which embeds it in your consciousness until that knowledge is natural and automatic. When you were a child and performed these rituals, it might have been with your classroom group and, unknowingly, you were supporting while challenging one another to internalize those sets of information quickly so you could move on to the next great challenge.

Religious institutions also use rituals. They do it to pass on information, as well, but there is a second important reason for them to use rituals. There is spiritual comfort in ritual, a sense of connection to the divine. That comfort is an important part of worship and feeling community within your religious institution. It opens you up to receive the experience of the Mass or service and opens your heart to lessons and messages.

Before moving on, it is important to draw a distinction between rituals and habits.

They are very different creatures. We might have a habit of biting our fingernails or double-checking to see that the door is locked. Brushing our teeth is a daily habit. But these actions don't serve to open us up or bring comfort. They are consistent actions, but the attitude or the consciousness may be random. Habits can be mindless, but rituals are always mindful.

Prosperity Practices are financially related activities done with a deliberate spiritual mindset. You are likely already engaged in money rituals that may or may not be working for you. If every time you sit down to pay your bills you feel angry at your spouse for leaving you to shoulder the responsibility alone, and you do that on the 15th and 30th of each month, that's a ritual. You're having a consistent action with an attitude that's probably not working to create intimacy or to move the family finances forward.

Or maybe you are a business owner who enjoys sitting back with her favorite beverage and reviewing the sales activity of the past week, feeling excited about new clients and appreciating the effort of your team. That's a consistent action with a chosen mindset that is likely creating momentum for success. Your goal for the most effective rituals is to have consistent repeated actions with a chosen attitude that moves you forward.

Take a moment to consider the rituals you have surrounding your money today. They might be related to looking for work and projects, paying bills, taxes, investing, savings or growing a business. Do you sigh with dread when you open up invoices hurriedly? Or do you plan ahead to bless every vendor who offers you services as you set up payments? Awareness of the financial actions you are taking and the spiritual attitudes you are engaging in is powerful.

"What are my current money rituals? How are these rituals working for me now?"

Guidance from a mentor and community support are important parts of the Prosperity Practices. What I have discovered after almost a decade of acting as a spiritual money mentor is that spiritual seekers thrive when they receive specific spiritual teaching around financial issues. Having a mentor who is a specialist in money and spirituality has been valuable in helping people to create and sustain Prosperity Practices that work for them.

The idea behind having community or social support, or a group of like-minded people to support you, is that you have an outlet for sharing your journey with others. Support of a group means that each of us has other people in our lives with whom we are sharing our goals and celebrating steps toward achieving those goals. Community support also provides us with necessary accountability and challenge.

A support group is important because it spurs you on to do your best. You may want to show yourself at your best when reporting on your progress or maybe you learn how to deeply feel the celebration of another person's achievements for the first time. Everyone is lifted up. Social support can provide the push we all need on occasion to stay the course and keep moving ahead. The accountability to the group can also keep you from rationalizing procrastination or less-than-optimal decisions.

Because we believe strongly in a support group and know that not everyone has one where they live, we have created *The Money Keys* Community. We have created a virtual community of people all over the world dedicated to spiritual growth and financial expansion. It's been a pleasure to see, first-hand, the transformation and support this kind of group can offer.

Weekly Activity

Our time, energy, and attention is powerful when we invest in weekly activity to accelerate our results. We know that a ritual is a consistent, repeated action with a selected consciousness or attitude. The reason that ritual will work for you is that you are already powerful and this is a way to focus that power.

When you put your time, energy and attention into something, you're going to get a good return. This is especially true if you're putting it into a desire for more spiritual faith. You're going to end up being more faithful and feel more spiritually connected because of your devotion. If you put that same energy into greater financial expansion, which could mean income growth, debt reduction or higher savings, you'll be able to accelerate your results.

We believe that you'll get the outcomes you desire more quickly if you're focused on them. You can complete your Prosperity Practice in a relatively short time each Monday and Friday and experience greater clarity, focus, appreciation and joy. As a result, you are going to get more done for your family, in your profession, with your finances, your money, and with your professional and business projects. You get both spiritual and financial goodies!

We chose Monday and Friday because that combination reflects the working rhythm in North America and much of the world. Monday is a great day for focus in our experience. It is the start of a new week and there's a sense that it is the day when we make our intentional decisions. Friday is the day for completion. Traditionally, it is the day on which we reflect on the week and finish projects. The rhythm and energy of these days can be very powerful.

Leverage the Masculine and Feminine

The Prosperity Practices are built on the infinite creativity of the masculine and feminine working together. Most people are familiar with the masculine and feminine symbols like the ones pictured here. Within each of us there is a unity of masculine and feminine qualities and energies. Masculine and feminine work together effectively and successfully in our beings and our wealth.

Masculine and feminine qualities of being can be found in wealth. The key in wealth-building, as within leading our lives, is to appreciate both. When the masculine and feminine are both valued and leveraged, everybody benefits, no matter what your gender. Neither quality is positive. Neither quality is negative. The qualities are different, and each offers its own unique traits.

A masculine approach to wealth includes the spiritual qualities of power, clarity, direction and action. Masculine money focus helps you grow through action. Feminine qualities of wealth are love, grace, receptivity and awareness. Feminine spiritual faith helps you grow through awareness.

What we discovered when we established the Prosperity Practices, and saw people using them, is that they are a wonderful way to leverage the times you want to be engaged with action or focus with the times when you want to be more aware and faithful. They allow you to appreciate both masculine and feminine qualities of your own wealth.

Your Big Why

Money Focus Monday & Spiritual Faith Friday

Money Focus Monday and Spiritual Faith Friday work for everyone. It doesn't matter if you're a new entrepreneur, experienced business owner or empty-nester investor. It makes no difference if you're taking part in these days because of your family finances or if you're part of a team inside a company. Money Focus Monday and Spiritual Faith Friday can both be customized for you!

The Prosperity Practices can be modified to meet your needs and goals. When you set your intentions for the week, or when you do your spiritual giving, you do it for whatever your lifestyle might be. The Prosperity Practices work because they're designed for increasing focus and faith that can apply to a wide variety of financial situations.

As we mention flexibility, we should recognize that while there is flexibility in the Prosperity Practices depending on your goals, we do recommend accountability for everyone. In our global Money Keys Community, we typically share our Money Focus Monday and Spiritual Faith Friday intentions and gratitude in our private online group. It works very well because we're celebrating and accountable to one another. You can choose intentions and gratitude on your own, but be mindful of how powerful it is to share with a partner, team, mastermind group or a mentor.

Creating Your Big Why Statement

When I was first visioning for *The Money Keys* ministry and book, one of the phrases that emerged was, "It's not about the money… it's: 'What's the money for?' " When people discover their own answer to that question, they can create an intention or a statement for themselves. That spiritual statement grows bigger and better while the individual moves forward financially. It's not just about the money.

Every month or so the bank sends us a statement of our accounts. That statement tells us where our money has been and where it is going. Your Big Why Statement is a spiritual statement about your personal wealth journey. In both cases, the statement tells us about our financial past, present and future.

The first element needed for you to create your Big Why Statement is to craft your own answer to, "What's the money for?" That answer will be different for everyone. Think carefully about what you feel called to do in your life and how money supports those dreams.

Here is an example of a Big Why Statement:

"I, Mary, see myself as a vital leader of Holistic Healing Unlimited. We inspire our clients into their vibrant health as our practice grows in reach, revenue and reputation this year. Divine Grace expresses as client service, marketing and team engagement. Top line revenue grows by 25 percent and more each quarter as we increase client cross sell, prospecting activities and number of affiliate partners. We all thrive!"

Creating Your Statement

You'll be creating a spiritual statement for your money life. It's your answer to "What's the money for?" We've found that one of the easiest methods for doing this is to start simply.

My Why: "What's the money for?"

- Choose a verb and a noun that summarize what you're up to in your life. It should be a simple, active phrase that connects you to your mission, your values, your professional life or your money life.

- You'll probably want to include increasing, decreasing or improving something in your statement. An example would be: "I want to grow my business with joy."
  - Increase________________________
  - Decrease _______________________
  - Improve_________________________
- It's helpful to begin your spiritual statement with phrases about yourself, such as:
  - I lead…
  - I serve…
  - I create…

So that you can have a frame of reference, in the Mary example, her statement is, "I, Mary, see myself as a vital leader of Holistic Healing Unlimited. We inspire our clients into their vibrant health as our practice grows in reach, revenue and reputation this year." Mary is leading Holistic Healing Unlimited and wants to grow (increase) revenue and reputation.

Your statement can be very simple as in the example, "I want to grow my business with joy." It can also be very specific if there are specific needs. For example, "I will resolve my father's estate with love by the end of the year." Finally, your statement can be very general, "Shift my relationship with money from childhood resistance to being a masterful, joyous financial adult." Often the simpler the statement, the better.

Once you've determined what you'd most like to increase or improve, when you can clearly define who or what you serve, you can wordsmith your statement to make it perfect. Begin by just focusing on your elements of growth and leadership.

Let's look more deeply at Mary's statement compared with the elements needed to answer the question, "What's the money for?" We told you to choose your verb and noun. Mary wants to grow her practice. Then we told you to create a spiritual statement with a phrase about yourself. Mary says, "I see myself as a vital leader…" She might have also started that sentence with "I lead…"

Take some time to consider your own spiritual statement for your money. Feel free to use Mary's statement as an example. Remember, begin by getting your ideas, verbs and nouns down on paper. You can always go back and adjust your statement later if need be.

What Spiritual Quality am I Deepening in?

A spiritual quality is an attribute of God or the divine. Spiritual quality implies a quality of being, an unconditional aspect of creation. Some examples are Love, Grace, Freedom, Wisdom, Peace, Joy, Wholeness, Abundance, Truth, Beauty and Power. As you craft your Big Why statement, it is important to think about the spiritual quality you'll be deepening in when you use it in relationship to your Prosperity Practice.

'What spiritual quality am I deepening in?'

When you are able to learn about, commune, practice and understand a spiritual quality, you are pulling out of yourself, or evoking, the God qualities in you. You are evoking the highest of who you are. An example might be if you asked, "What would Love do here?" Asking this question would be accessing an unconditional and spiritual quality.

Let's review some additional examples of a spiritual quality. Cheerfulness is a human mood, but Joy is a spiritual quality. There's always more Joy to be explored, discovered and expressed.

Other spiritual qualities could be:

- Love reveals in me as I build my business.

- I joyously live in the Grace of God as I complete and resolve all the financial obligations from our real estate investments.
- I welcome Freedom expressing as I create joint venture partnerships that absolutely express the good of God.

What Financial Goals am I Committed to?

A goal is a mark or a measure that inspires you to move forward. We already have and are the fullness of the divine. We express through things such as revenue growth the fullness that we already are by doing things such as increasing the number of prospecting conversations we are having. It might be easy to place a positive or negative connotation on these goals, but that isn't their purpose. For example, "My sales are bad now, but they're going to get better." Instead, think of these goals as a way of tracking and celebrating your experience of growing with the divine.

'What are my financial goals?'

Financial goals include things you'd like to increase or decrease. You may want to increase your income or decrease your debt. These goals don't have to include every detail you might track in your business or your personal finances. Rather, they are the headlines – the most important measurements.

We like to measure our financial goals as a way of fully embracing our experience. To do this we use Process and Results Measures. Process Measures look at the steps to accomplish goals, the process or the speed, and can include qualitative measures such as "My beloved and I handle weekly financial tasks with joy and humor." This is a statement with goals that you can measure quantitatively and qualitatively. Did you have fewer fights? More happiness? Process Measures could include the sequence of actions that are taken to accomplish your goals. For example, "Did I make three prospecting calls and follow up with one proposal?"

'How will I measure results?'

Results Measures are the things you can calculate at the end of a period of time. These tend to be mostly quantitative measurements. They will include numbers and percentages. Here are a few examples:

- How much money is in the portfolio?
- Our revenue is growing by__ % each__ .
- How many prospects do we have?
- What is the dollar per client engagement needed to reduce debt or negotiate rates?

Keep in mind that Results Measures are tangible and can be counted. When you're setting your goals, if you're using phrases such as "debt reduced," "rates re-negotiated" or "expenses streamlined," you're on the right track. They are milestones or accomplishments that you are able to point to as measures of your success.

An example of financial goals for Mary might be that her top-line revenue will increase by 25 percent or more each quarter. Mary is also tracking revenue weekly and monthly to see progress toward her quarterly goals. Each week and month, she will evaluate the increase in client cross-sale and prospecting activities in a number of affiliate partners. These are measurable. Take some time to consider your financial goals and measures.

An example of a spiritual statement that includes financial goals is, "I, Bruce, serve a powerful vision of prosperous living for me and my family built on Creativity. I am competent, intelligent and open to grow as a real estate investor. Each week, I will research three to five opportunities, learn one or more new tools, meet two or more potential clients or partners and build my capacity. I welcome one or more new projects launched and one or more completed purchases in the next 90 to 120 days."

Your spiritual statement will be unique to you and your personal goals. You may decide you'd like to rearrange the words a bit, but if you've followed along, you've created a strong foundation for your final statement. Once you've answered the question, "What's the money for?" and determined spiritual qualities, financial goals and measures, you have the structure and substance that you'll need.

Money Focus Monday

Money Focus Monday is experiencing wealth through action. You'll probably recall our discussion of how wealth has masculine and feminine qualities. Monday is when you utilize the masculine money focus energy for the week.

The themes for Monday center on giving. You'll be giving attention to your wealth concerns. You will also be giving money in the form of spiritual giving or tithing.

Money Focus Monday practices leverage the masculine qualities of Power, Clarity and Action.

The Law of Circulation

Money Focus Monday works because of the spiritual principle and the Law of Circulation. A spiritual principle would be a truth that can be tested. Spiritual principles are found across all of the world's religious traditions. The Law of Circulation is the idea that all of life is giving and receiving and that together they create a flow. We use the infinity symbol to represent the Law of Circulation because we know that its vital flow never ends.

In healthy systems, there must be energetic exchange along the way. When circulation is cut off, the flow stops. For example, if you're asked to provide a good or service for free, without exchange, circulation gets cut off. Financial exchange is how we participate with the Law of Circulation.

When you ignore the Law of Circulation and stop the flow, difficulties arise. Just as in your own body, when there is a blockage in the flow of blood, you have serious health problems. When you have a break or blockage in your financial circulation, you can have financial health problems.

On Monday, you're conscious and deliberate about giving. On Friday, you're conscious and deliberate about receiving. You're creating a flow that honors the Law of Circulation. Strong circulation equates to vitality. Any system needs vitality, be it your body, a relationship, an organization or your financial system. It is that vitality that will support you in achieving success.

Money Focus Monday:

My Statement, Financial Tasks, Spiritual Giving, Sharing.

Let's consider the elements needed to honor the Law of Circulation and move toward our goals on Money Focus Monday.

- Statement. Say your spiritual statement of "What's the money for?" out loud and with passion. Really connect to the qualities and the energy of it.

- Financial Tasks. Give your attention to your money flows for the week. Monday is when you sit down and take financial actions that are relevant for you each week. If you are a business owner, you might be reviewing expenses or payroll. If you're managing your family finances, you might be paying bills, recording deposits or setting aside funds for upcoming events or other purchases. While you complete your financial tasks and transactions, you may say a prayer or put on beautiful music and be certain that you're making this practice both conscious and powerful.

When many people think about reviewing finances and paying bills, they plan to do it at the end of the week, perhaps on payday. Consider the effect of turning that thinking around. When you focus on your money and financial tasks on Monday, you open yourself up to receive for the remainder of the week. This is the best way to prepare yourself for a prosperous week and for your Spiritual Faith Friday ritual.

Many of the people that are attuned to this way of doing things are business owners or the main marketer for their team or group. So Money Focus Monday is also a time for them to give attention to potential sales that will close during the week. What new business will they bring onboard? Giving attention on Monday to where your income will be coming from is as important as determining where your money will be going.

- Spiritual Giving. Money Focus Monday is also significant because of spiritual giving or tithing. Sometimes people do this on a Sunday or Saturday at places of worship. Even if you gave another day, you are going to give it your attention on Monday. Spiritual giving is an opportunity to have a spiritual connection and a reminder of being in the presence of the divine, being in the flow.

Spiritual giving is a faith practice. It spans across all the world's religious traditions. When you take part in spiritual giving, the first thing you will do is to give thanks for the 100 percent you receive. Some people do this by going to their business accounts or personal accounts and looking for the deposits for the week and giving thanks for each of those. Giving thanks for the 100 percent you have received keeps you in the flow.

The next step is for you to share a percentage of your financial receipts through spiritual giving. You give a portion to the people, institutions and causes that inspire you. There's no wrong way to be a giver. Give thought to the people, artists, musicians or organizations that make you feel closer to God. Those are the places to give.

When you give 10 percent, that's called a tithe. Tithe literally means a tenth. Our encouragement is to begin with a consistent gracious percentage and go from there. Even if you can't give 10 percent, give something.

The benefits of being a spiritual giver are immediately felt in the generosity that you experience. We strongly recommend that you don't wait to give. Some people believe that they will wait to give until they have more money. The truth is that this element isn't about the amount of money you're giving, but the fact that you're giving something. Be a giver from the beginning.

When you choose to avoid spiritual giving, you are blocking the flow of Circulation. When you pay it forward, you open yourself up to receive.

- Intentions. Set your practical actions, or intentions, for the week on Monday. You've already said your statement out loud, which often guides you to places to take action. Make it a practice to view the goals as real, fresh and new each week.

Give attention to the tasks and the actions needed in order to move your financial goals forward. Choose no more than three to five things that will help you reach your goals. Then determine how you will measure your progress qualitatively and quantitatively. This process allows you to set yourself up for priority, focus and quality for the week. Go with quality, vibration and rising energy instead of quantity of tasks.

Some question what an action is. An action can be a decision you make, research you do, tasks that you either accomplish or delegate, or it could be a communication needed. Action can refer to many different things, but the goal is movement forward.

- Share and Support. The final Money Focus Monday element is to share your giving and intentions with your group, your team, your partner or your mentor. After you've done your spiritual giving or tithing, you can share the joy of giving with your support group. Let people know where you decided to give, if that feels comfortable for you. Support one another. Each week in our global spirituality and money community, we hear people say things such as, “When I tithe, I thrive.” Share what you have been giving attention to with your finances and set yourself up to be accountable for the actions you have chosen. This is an opportunity for you to be in a place of clarity with yourself and your support group. As a result of Money Focus Monday, you are focused, organized and set up for success.

Spiritual Faith Friday

You've made it through the week, focused on your action items, moving forward toward your final goals and arrived at Spiritual Faith Friday. Once again we value the masculine and feminine traits of wealth. The beautiful weekly rhythm allows us to set our intentions and take action on Monday before we build wealth through awareness on Friday.

Spiritual Faith Friday practices celebrate the feminine spiritual qualities of Grace, Inclusivity and Awareness.

Spiritual Faith Friday is about developing feminine spiritual faith through receptivity. On this day, we build our experience of wealth, wholeness and oneness with awareness practices. Fridays are when we are receptive. We focus on receiving and celebrating deliberately through our thoughts, emotions and spiritual connections. Honoring spiritual qualities in Prosperity Practices with Monday as focus and Friday as faith on a regular basis is very powerful.

The Law of Unity

The reason that Spiritual Faith Friday works is because of a spiritual principle called the Law of Unity. The Law of Unity is the idea that all of life is an interconnected whole. This concept is embraced across the world's religious traditions. It is the notion that the divine or the transcendent reality is love. It's at the center of who and what we are. So we celebrate our oneness in line with The Law of Unity. In it we know that everything we desire, we already are.

On Spiritual Faith Fridays, we spend our time, energy and attention in connection with the divine and with faith-building. When we build our faith, we are deepening our awareness, our experience and our ability to feel. We welcome our sense of oneness and union with the divine, that which we have and already are. We recognize that we are individualized expressions of God, or the divine. We already have and are the fullness of the divine.

Yet, this is a beautiful, paradoxical time. We're going to acknowledge new achievements, possessions and experiences. These "new things" are really expressions of the divine emerging from the fullness of who we already are. We celebrate the external in service of the infinite, internal, eternal truth.

Spiritual Faith Friday:

My Statement, Spiritual Qualities, Financial Goals, Sharing.

Let's consider the elements needed to honor the Law of Unity in a place of receptivity, knowing that all of life is interconnected.

- Statement. On Spiritual Faith Friday, say your statement of "What's the money for?" out loud and with passion. Make a point to really connect to it. Hear and internalize each word in your statement. Feel it resonate within you and allow it to take root.
- Reflection on Spiritual Qualities. Look back over your week and, in a journal or diary, remember and reflect on the spiritual qualities that you have chosen in your statement. How are they revealing themselves now through conversations, actions, feelings, decisions and events?

Take time to feel your oneness with God and take notice. This is the time for you to collect the evidence of how the spiritual qualities that you're really cultivating are revealing themselves through the activities of the week. Spiritual qualities may reveal themselves through conversations, actions, feelings, decisions or events.

There are many ways this can happen. Let's use Mary as an example again. The spiritual quality she is focused on is divine grace. Perhaps during the week, Mary was confronted by a difficult vendor situation but was able to find an easy resolution to it. She would appreciate that grace and take note of it.

You may notice simple things such as the fact that you had a sense of the divine when an email was answered beautifully or in a way that you couldn't have predicted. Perhaps you were focused on the spiritual quality of power. You may choose to record how you felt your own power and value when you handled yourself well in a difficult negotiation.

- Reflection on Financial Goals. Friday is also the time to look at your week and journal or reflect about how your financial goals are revealing now. Do this by collecting evidence that includes specific details, including Process and Results Measures. Embrace the ability to show that you're making progress to your final goals.

We can look back to Mary for an example. She might write in her journal, "I, Mary, attended three networking events, set up six prospecting conversations and converted two prospects into new clients. I feel present, joyous and graceful. I felt the grace of the divine while it was happening."

Deliberately looking for how your goals are manifesting is important to the overall journey because whatever we're interested in appreciates in our lives. What you focus on, appreciates. You're more interested in how your desires are here now than you are in complaining about what isn't happening.

Because you have the skill and awareness to see the spiritual qualities expressing, you're developing your capacity to discover them in the practical ways that your money life unfolds throughout the week.

- Share and Support. Just as we did on Monday, take time to share your experiences with your support group. Offer stories and accomplishments from your week to your group, team, partner or mentor. If you were challenged with taking action on an intention, what did you learn from that experience? On Friday, we share for the purpose of support, encouragement and celebration. Do this for yourself and for other members of your group each Spiritual Faith Friday. You'll complete your week energized, grateful and feeling more abundant.

Summary and Celebration

Congratulations, you have created a plan for anchoring your spiritual and financial expansion with weekly Prosperity Practices! When you do your weekly Prosperity Practices, they become rooted in your life and help you keep from drifting into doubt, victimization, upset or being overwhelmed by money. These rituals help you stay on track and moving toward your goals.

Depending on tasks, work, family and travel in your typical week, you may spend five to 10 minutes working on your ritual, or you may invest 30 to 45 minutes. How long it takes is irrelevant, what matters is that you are experiencing each part of your Wealth Ritual and engaging fully in Money Focus Monday and Spiritual Faith Friday. We have some folks in *The Money Keys* Community who do their Money Focus Monday on Superfocused Sunday and do Spiritual Faith Friday on Sacred Saturday. They get their maximum benefit because those days work for their lives.

It is important that you engage with your Prosperity Practices consistently. If you miss one, forgive yourself, and pick it up again the following week. The principles, the Law of Unity and the Law of Circulation, don't take time off even if you do. They are going to be active and working for you all the time. You don't have to do anything to make them work! Your Money Focus Monday and Spiritual Faith Friday, along with your choices to participate in your Prosperity Practices and all associated activities, help you to put yourself in alignment with what the principles are already doing. They help you maximize the spiritual resources you already have!

Online Bonus Tools

We are so appreciative that you have read this book and that you are engaged in the Prosperity Practices. We want to provide you with some additional tools and ideas for continuing your spiritual and financial expansion. Please visit our Prosperity Practices Bonus page at www.MoneyKeysPractices.com, where you will see a video welcome message and overview by Reverend Karen, some additional worksheets as well as audio guides to use on Money Focus Monday and Spiritual Faith Friday.

Plus, there you'll discover three special bonuses from the hundreds of tools in the online Money Keys Community library. The first is the Guerrilla Gratitude Practice, a guided exercise for eliciting appreciation for everything in your financial experience. The second is Financial Forgiveness, a powerful tool for setting yourself free from upsets of past financial pain. And you'll receive a third bonus: Money Management System, a spiritually oriented way to establish a financial plan for income growth, debt reduction and savings.

About the Author

Rev. Karen Russo, MBA, is a money and spirituality expert and spiritual leader of the global Money Keys Community. She's the award-winning author of *The Money Keys: Unlocking Peace, Freedom and Real Financial Power,* endorsed by her teachers, Dr. Michael Bernard Beckwith and Katherine Woodward Thomas, with a foreword by Bob Proctor.

Karen brings an unusual blend of 25 years of experiences and insights as a top-selling salesperson and leadership and sales trainer for the Fortune 500 with an MBA from Columbia University and a Masters of Consciousness Studies as an ordained interfaith minister.

She's featured in a provocative chapter in Sharon Lechter's *Think and Grow Rich for*

Women, in the movie series *The Second Fifty*, on TV's Fox News and in The Arizona Republic.

Karen is passionate about showing business owners, creative professionals and spiritual seekers that the world needs us at our best: peaceful, creative, generous, prosperous and free!

Karen lives in the American Southwest with her beloved Bill and celebrated her 50th birthday by running the Phoenix Marathon.

Notes